R. VAUGHAN WILLIAMS

FANTASIA

FOR PIANO AND ORCHESTRA

PIANO AND ORCHESTRAL REDUCTION
(TWO PIANOS)

EDITED BY

GRAHAM PARLETT

MUSIC DEPARTMENT

OXFORD
UNIVERSITY PRESS

OXFORD
UNIVERSITY PRESS

Great Clarendon Street, Oxford OX2 6DP,
United Kingdom

Oxford University Press is a department of the University of Oxford.
It furthers the University's objective of excellence in research, scholarship,
and education by publishing worldwide. Oxford is a registered trade mark of
Oxford University Press in the UK and in certain other countries

This Edition published with the kind support of The Vaughan Williams Charitable Trust

The right of Ralph Vaughan Williams to be named as the Composer of this Work has been asserted
in accordance with the Copyright, Designs and Patents Act, 1988

First published 2012

Impression: 1

ISBN 978-0-19-338826-0

Music origination by Katie Johnston
Printed in Great Britain on acid-free paper by
Halstan & Co. Ltd, Amersham, Bucks.

Full scores and orchestral parts are available on hire from the publisher.
A full score containing full description of the editorial method
is also available as a study score, ISBN 978–0–19–338825–3.

PREFACE

In 1895, after taking his Mus. Bac. and B.A. degrees at Cambridge, Vaughan Williams returned to the Royal College of Music in order to study composition with Charles Villiers Stanford, and it was here that he met Gustav Holst, who was to become his greatest musical friend. In October of the following year, the month in which he celebrated his twenty-fourth birthday, he began work on the *Fantasia*, his earliest known piece for a solo instrument with orchestra. By the time he completed its final revision, in October 1904, exactly eight years later, he had discovered English folksong, embarked on *A Sea Symphony*, and completed a number of other works that are now well known, such as 'Linden Lea', *In the Fen Country*, *The House of Life*, and *Songs of Travel*, as well as several scores that have recently been revived for publication, including *The Garden of Proserpine*, his doctoral mass (published as *A Cambridge Mass*), and *Heroic Elegy and Triumphal Epilogue*.

There is no dedication on the score of the *Fantasia*, nor is it known whether Vaughan Williams wrote it with any particular pianist in mind or ever tried to have it performed. It may have been among the compositions that he showed to Holst on one of their regular 'field days', when they would meet to discuss and criticize each other's work in progress. The title appears in a list of 'My "most important works"' that he sent to the critic Edwin Evans in about June 1903 (i.e. before its final revision), but there are no further references to it in his correspondence, and after its donation in 1960 to the Department of Manuscripts of the British Museum (now British Library) it languished in obscurity for another fifty years. In 2010 the pianist Mark Bebbington learned of its existence and inspected the manuscript. Although he could detect the influence of composers such as Franck, Liszt, Scriabin, and Brahms, he concluded that it contained many characteristic hallmarks of the later Vaughan Williams. Bebbington recorded the work with the Ulster Orchestra and conductor George Vass at a session for Somm Recordings in the Ulster Hall, Belfast, on 16 May 2011. The CD (SOMMCD246) was released in October, with the title given as *Fantasy* rather than *Fantasia*.

In spite of the influences noted above, the score contains many passages that foreshadow the composer in his maturity, perhaps the most characteristic being the ones involving the chorale-like melody that begins at bar 15, forms the basis of the scherzo section (365 ff.), and returns in full glory towards the end (471 ff.). Michael Kennedy has also pointed out pre-echoes of the *Fantasia on the 'Old 104th' Psalm Tune* for piano, chorus, and orchestra, written half a century later. This score, the three-movement concerto that he wrote for Harriet Cohen in the late 1920s, and the earlier *Fantasia* are Vaughan Williams's only pieces for solo piano and orchestra.

GRAHAM PARLETT
2012

TEXTUAL NOTES

This edition of the *Fantasia*, with the orchestral part arranged for a second piano, is based on the holograph full-score manuscript. Editorial emendations to the solo part are detailed below. References are to bar numbers. RH = right hand; LH = left hand.

50   RH, 3rd beat: this is a crotchet in the MS but has been changed to a quaver, as in the surrounding bars.

70   RH scale: this is written in the MS as a group of 28 demisemiquavers. The LH scale is written as 21 demisemiquavers plus a separate semiquaver sextuplet. These have been corrected to 21 demisemiquavers in both hands followed by a semiquaver septuplet in the RH and a sextuplet in the LH.

75   RH, 3rd beat: this is a quaver in the MS but has been changed to a crotchet, as in the surrounding bars.

245   LH, last note: this is unclear in the MS but looks like B♭ corrected from G.

270–9 RH: the slur is not in the MS but bar 279 has the continuation of a slur after a page turn. The two preceding pages had been jettisoned leaving only the stubs, but in its new, truncated form the passage (marked *legato*) seems to call for a slur.

359   LH, 2nd beat: the upper note is B in the MS, not A or C as in the RH.

399   There is no quaver chord in this bar (unlike 401–3); this is probably intentional, not an oversight.

415   The bracketed '3' in both hands indicates that there are three beats in the bar, not four, as previously; it does not indicate a triplet. The sextuplets have '3' rather than '6' in the MS. The LH B (thus stemmed) is clearly written. The preceding E appears twice, in the LH, then in the RH, but the first is here omitted as the group is a sextuplet not a septuplet.

420   LH chord: this is erroneously preceded by a bass clef in the MS.

427   The first notes are thus stemmed in the MS.

441   LH, 1st beat: the 2nd note (D) of the quintuplet seems to have an A written above it in the MS. This is clearly a mistake and is omitted.

442   RH, 2nd beat: the last note of the quintuplet may be an E rather than D, as given here; the MS is unclear.

478   LH, 1st beat: the top note is E in the MS, not D as in the orchestral parts (though not at this pitch level). It may or may not be a mistake.

494   Both hands: the Cs and Gs lack sharps in the MS but these are presumably intended.

Duration: *c.*21 minutes

Fantasia
for piano and orchestra

Orchestral reduction
by Graham Parlett

R. VAUGHAN WILLIAMS

OXFORD UNIVERSITY PRESS, MUSIC DEPARTMENT, GREAT CLARENDON STREET, OXFORD OX2 6DP

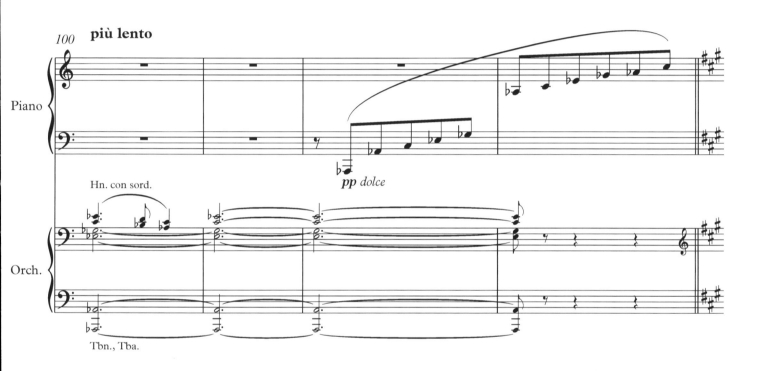

un pochettino allargando

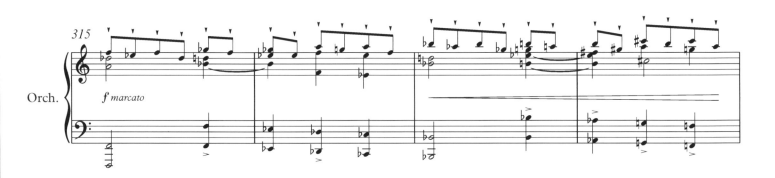

28 **poco accelerando**

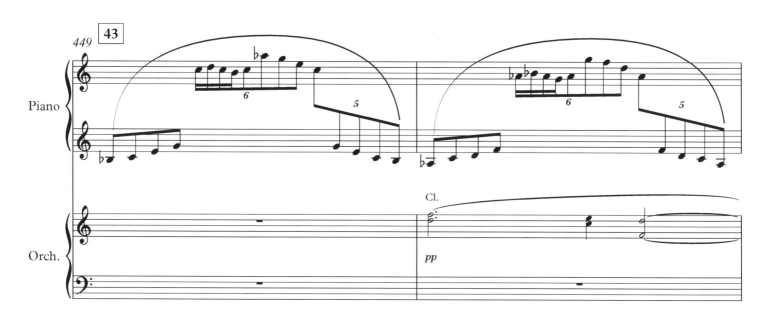

44

Quasi Cadenza